HAVDALAH

THE CEREMONY THAT COMPLETES THE SABBATH

NEIL AND JAMIE LASH

Lederer Books
a division of
Messianic Jewish Publishers
Clarksville, Maryland

Unless otherwise noted, Scripture quotations are taken from:

Complete Jewish Bible © 1998 by David H. Stern
Published by Jewish New Testament Publications, Inc.

Printed in the United States of America

Cover Design by
Josh Huhn, Design Point, Inc.
Layout Design by
Valerie Levy, Drawing Board Studios

14 13 12   4 3 2

ISBN 978-1-880226-60-5

Library of Congress Catalog Control Number: 2009920574

Lederer Books
A division of
MESSIANIC JEWISH PUBLISHERS
6120 Day Long Lane
Clarksville, MD 21029

Distributed by
Messianic Jewish Resources International
Order line: (800) 410-7367
E-mail: Lederer@messianicjewish.net
Website: www.messianicjewish.net

CONTENTS

INTRODUCTION

Messianic Judaism is a relatively new movement in the religious community that began to blossom in the 1970s and has spread throughout the world. Today, there are Messianic congregations in most major cities in the United States and in many foreign nations as well, with at least 100 congregations in Israel.

Local leaders are establishing traditions within Messianic Judaism as they decide which Jewish traditions are consistent with Messianic Jewish theology, to be incorporated into a Messianic lifestyle. Some traditions, such as Passover *seders*, are thoroughly based in the bible, and congregants can easily accept them. Others, such as *havdalah*, a simple, short ceremony that concludes the Sabbath, call for further study. The exploration contained within these pages is an example of how each tradition could be examined before Messianic congregations adopt it as their own.

In this brief study, you will learn about havdalah—the tradition behind it, the ceremony itself, and how it relates to followers of Yeshua. You will have all the information you need for a new family tradition that will help you enjoy the Sabbath and understand more about your relationship with *Yeshua HaMashiach* (Jesus the Messiah).

CHAPTER 1

THE TRADITION
BEHIND HAVDALAH

Although havdalah is not directly mentioned in the Scriptures, its inherent meaning is based on an important scriptural truth—separation between the sacred and secular. In havdalah, we have the potential of making this truth more tangible, accessible, and consistent with the Jewish roots of our faith in Messiah.

Havdalah—the ceremony that signifies and focuses us on the end of *Shabbat* (the Sabbath) and the beginning of the new week—was first instituted around the fourth century BCE by the *soferim*, the scribes of the Second Temple, who were collectively known as "the Men of the Great Assembly." It was originally part of the *Amidah* synagogue prayer at the conclusion of the Sabbath and later became a home celebration "for the benefit of the children" (Berakhot 5:2). Like many of the ceremonies connected with the Feasts of the Lord, havdalah involves the five senses to explain religious concepts, with special emphasis on teaching the children. Consider the Passover elements and the biblical injunction in Exodus, "When your children ask you, 'What do you mean by this ceremony?' Say, 'It is the sacrifice of ADONAI's Pesach [Passover]...'" Exodus 12:26–27a.

SEPARATED UNTO GOD

One of God's greatest gifts to his people is the Sabbath, which families welcome each Friday evening, as if they were escorting a blushing bride down the aisle. There is joy, expectation, and holiness in the moment, and like the celebration after the wedding, the weekend is also a celebration. Each Saturday evening, the Sabbath is ushered out with havdalah, which is neither a requirement nor a law. It is a way of meaningfully ending the Shabbat. Aside from being a gift from God, the Sabbath is also a sign to his people Israel (Exod. 31), as well as the first feast of the Lord (Lev. 23:3). Havdalah helps people enjoy the Shabbat as long as possible. It is so intimately connected with Shabbat that we cannot look at one without reflecting on the other. The Hebrew word havdalah means "separation" or "division," thus, the havdalah ceremony highlights the separation between Shabbat and the rest of the week.

The ceremony affirms the separation between the sacred and the secular, between light and darkness, and between Israel and the Nations. Havdalah is a tradition that proclaims: There are moral distinctions in the universe; there is a right way and a wrong way; there is God's way and man's way.

The root meaning of the word "holy" (Heb.: *kadosh*) is separation. Just as holy describes the very nature of God, it should describe God's people as well. When God chooses a people, he separates them from all other people by his presence. In a beautiful dialogue between God and Moses, this separation of Israel is clearly expressed:

> For how else is it to be known that I have found favor in your sight, I and your people, other than by your going with us? That is what distinguishes us, me and your people, from all the other peoples on earth. ADONAI said to Moshe, "I will also do what you have asked me to do, because you have found favor in my sight, and I know you by name." (Exod. 33:16–17)

God called Israel to be a holy nation: distinct, separate, chosen, and special. Consecration was never an option; it was an integral part of God's calling and of the love relationship between God and Israel, like a marriage. The people of God are to be the "garden locked up" of Song of Solomon 4:12—the private property or guarded jewel that is set apart for the pleasure of the Beloved.

Although exiled because Israel at-large failed to fulfill its side of the covenant, there were those within Israel who were faithful. Their faithfulness made others still view the Jewish People as distinct. Daniel and his friends refused the choicest foods from King Nebuchadnezzar's table to maintain the consecration of their bodies to their God (Dan. 1). Through their obedience, God brought favor on Daniel and his friends and they quickly rose to prominence in the king's court. During the reign of King

Ahasuerus of Persia, Haman, the second in command and an enemy of the Jewish People, told the king:

> There is a particular people scattered and dispersed among the peoples in all the provinces of your kingdom. Their laws are different from those of every other people... (Esther 3:8)

This kind of holiness and separation brought persecution and rejection, as evidenced in the book of Esther and in the lives of Daniel and his three friends (Dan. 3, 6), but God defended those who lived for him. Those promises remain true for all followers of the Messiah as well.

The emissary Peter called believers to this lifestyle when he wrote:

> On the contrary, following the Holy One who called you, become holy yourselves in your entire way of life; since the Tanakh says, "You are to be holy because I am holy." (1 Pet. 1:15–16)

This is a complete commitment to what God has called us to when we believe in him. It is something that follows us throughout our day, our week, our lives. It is not confined to a location or a day on the calendar.

The manifold blessing of God upon his children is directly related to their holy living and separation unto him. This is the tradition behind havdalah, embraced through its enactment and how it connects us to the separate and holy calling of our people—centuries ago and even now.

CHAPTER 2

THE CEREMONY

We usher out the Shabbat—a separate day of rest, reflection, and relaxation in the Lord (as well as a picture of the eternal rest promised to all believers in Hebrews 4)—with fanfare. Just as Shabbat begins with candlelight, wine, and prayer, we introduce its departure with candlelight, wine, and prayer. The celebration can begin any time after night falls on Saturday. In some homes, parents encourage the children to watch for the first three stars in the evening sky, which signal that the Sabbath is over and that it's time for havdalah. Orthodox Jews celebrate havdalah immediately after the head of the family has returned home from the *Ma-ariv* (evening) service at the synagogue.

Before Beginning

You'll need the following items in order to celebrate havdalah

1. Havdalah candle
2. Kiddush cup and saucer
3. Wine or grape juice
4. Spice box with spices
5. Bible

Lighting the Candle

The havdalah ceremony begins with light. According to tradition, we do not kindle light on the Sabbath; therefore, the proper first use of light after Shabbat is for religious purposes, recalling the first act of the Creation when God said, "Let there be light" (Gen. 1:3).

The head of the household lights a special candle before the havdalah ceremony begins. The candle can be bought in Judaica shops (see related resources p. 28) or made by heating two long, thin candles and twisting them together. The minimum requirement for a havdalah candle is that it has at least two wicks. The ones we use are usually blue and white with four to eight wicks. Remember, the bigger the flame, the more dramatic and exciting it is!

A child usually holds the havdalah candle as all gather around a table. This can be an awesome experience for a young child. (Some care needs to be taken with the hot dripping wax.) Another option is to begin with the candle in a holder.

THE BLESSING OVER THE CANDLES

The head of household recites a blessing over the light of the havdalah candle.

בָּרוּךְ אַתָּה יְיָ אֱלֹהֵינוּ מֶלֶךְ הָעוֹלָם.
בּוֹרֵא מְאוֹרֵי הָאֵשׁ:

Transliteration: *Baruch atah Adonai Eloheynu Melech ha-olam borey m'orey ha-eysh.*

Translation: *Blessed art Thou, O Lord our God, King of the universe, who creates the light of the fire.*

While this blessing is recited, the head of the household usually spreads his or her hands toward the light as if to examine them—so as to make some use of the light and thereby justify the reciting of a blessing over it.

As Messianic believers, a good initial use of the light (and beginning of the new week) is to examine the Word of God. Here is where the head of the household could hold up a Bible to the light of the candle and read a few words from it.

RECITING THE SCRIPTURES

The head of the household recites the following prayer based on the Holy Scriptures in Hebrew and/or English:

הִנֵּה אֵל יְשׁוּעָתִי אֶבְטַח וְלֹא אֶפְחָד כִּי עָזִּי
וְזִמְרָת יָהּ יְיָ וַיְהִי-לִי לִישׁוּעָה: וּשְׁאַבְתֶּם מַיִם
בְּשָׂשׂוֹן מִמַּעַיְנֵי הַיְשׁוּעָה: לַייָ הַיְשׁוּעָה עַל-עַמְּךָ
בִּרְכָתֶךָ סֶּלָה: יְיָ צְבָאוֹת עִמָּנוּ מִשְׂגָּב-לָנוּ אֱלֹהֵי
יַעֲקֹב סֶלָה: לַיְהוּדִים הָיְתָה אוֹרָה וְשִׂמְחָה
וְשָׂשֹׂן וִיקָר: כֵּן תִּהְיֶה לָּנוּ: כּוֹס יְשׁוּעוֹת
אֶשָּׂא וּבְשֵׁם יְיָ אֶקְרָא:

Transliteration: Hiney Eyl y'shu'ati evtach v'lo efchad ki azi v'zimrat Yah Adonai va-y' hi'li lishu'a. Ushavtem mayim b'sason mima'ainey ha-y'shu'a l'Adonai ha-y'shu'a al-amcha birchatecha sela. Adonai tz'va'ot imanu misgav-lanu Elohai Ya'akov sela. La-Y'hudim haita ora v'simcha v'sason vikar. Keyn tih'yeh lanu. Kos y'shu'ot eh-sa Uvsheym Adonai ekra.

Translation: Behold, God is my salvation; I will trust and will not be afraid for God, the Lord, is my strength and song; he also has become my salvation. Therefore, with joy you will draw water from the wells of salvation. Salvation belongs to the Lord. Your blessing is upon your people. The Lord of Hosts is with us; the God of Jacob is our refuge. The Jews had light and gladness, joy and honor. So be it with us. I will take up the cup of salvation and call upon the Name of the Lord.

THE BLESSING OVER THE WINE

The next portion of the ceremony focuses on a cup of wine, central to most Jewish celebrations. During havdalah, a kiddush (blessing) cup holds the fruit of the vine (grape juice or wine). The head of household pours the wine until it overflows the cup's edges. Then he or she holds it in the right hand and blesses it as follows:

בָּרוּךְ אַתָּה יְיָ אֱלֹהֵינוּ מֶלֶךְ הָעוֹלָם,
בּוֹרֵא פְּרִי הַגָּפֶן:

Transliteration: *Baruch atah Adonai Eloheynu Melech ha-olam borey p'ri ha-gafen.*

Translation: *Blessed art Thou, O Lord our God, King of the universe, who creates the fruit of the vine.*

Young children, who are often cautioned about not spilling, are especially enthralled as they watch the liquid pour over the edges. Spilling is not only allowed, it is encouraged. It is a must during havdalah to express the joy, symbolized by wine, we received during the Sabbath.

THE BLESSING OVER THE SPICES

Next comes the *b'samim* (spices), which represent the sweetness of Shabbat. Usually cloves or cinnamon are kept in a small, decorated box, which will be passed around so everyone can inhale their fragrant aroma. The containers are made of silver, brass, or wood and can be either very simple or artistic creations. The most popular design for the spice box over the years has been that of a tower, similar to the tower of a castle. Today, there is every imaginable design for spice boxes as a result of a revival in Jewish ritual and synagogue art.

In our home, we use a simple brass spice box filled with whole cloves and cinnamon sticks. Some use flowers, even rose water, instead of spices.

A child also customarily holds the b'samim. The head of the household takes the spice box from the child who is holding it and says the following:

בָּרוּךְ אַתָּה יְיָ אֱלֹהֵינוּ מֶלֶךְ הָעוֹלָם. בּוֹרֵא מִינֵי בְשָׂמִים:

Transliteration: *Baruch atah Adonai Eloheynu Melech ha-olam, borey miney b'samim.*

Translation: *Blessed art Thou, O Lord our God, King of the universe, who creates various kinds of spices.*

The family then passes around the spice box to smell the fragrance, sharing the aroma of Shabbat with others. Anyone can offer a spontaneous prayer at this point that the Lord would carry the fragrance of Shabbat into the new week. Another person can pray that the Sabbath rest in Messiah might be a reality each day, as well as a petition that the lives of those present might be a love song to the Messiah.

THE HAVDALAH BLESSING

The head of household takes the cup of wine again in the right hand as the havdalah ceremony concludes with a special blessing emphasizing the theme of being set apart.

בָּרוּךְ אַתָּה יְיָ אֱלֹהֵינוּ מֶלֶךְ הָעוֹלָם.
הַמַּבְדִּיל בֵּין קֹדֶשׁ לְחוֹל בֵּין אוֹר לְחֹשֶׁךְ
בֵּין יִשְׂרָאֵל לָעַמִּים. בֵּין יוֹם הַשְּׁבִיעִי
לְשֵׁשֶׁת יְמֵי הַמַּעֲשֶׂה. בָּרוּךְ אַתָּה יְיָ
הַמַּבְדִּיל בֵּין קֹדֶשׁ לְחוֹל.

Transliteration: *Baruch atah Adonai Eloheynu Melech ha-olam, hamavdil beyn kodesh l'chol beyn or l'choshech beyn Yisrael la-amin beyn yom ha-sh'vi' i l'sheyshet y'mey ha-ma'aseh. Baruch atah Adonai hamavdil beyn-kodesh l'chol.*

Translation: *Blessed art Thou, O Lord our God, King of the universe, who makes a distinction between holy and profane, between light and darkness, between Israel and the heathen nations, between the seventh day and the six working days. Blessed are you, O Lord, who makes a distinction between holy and profane.*

All present now partake of the fruit of the vine.

THE CANDLE IS EXTINGUISHED

The head of the household extinguishes the havdalah candle in the wine that was spilled over into the saucer. The *Authorized Daily Prayer Book* tells us:

… we have *seen* the symbols of havdalah.
… we have *tasted* the wine.
… we have *smelled* the fragrant spices.
… we have *felt* the heat of the flame.
… and we have *heard* the Word of the Lord. (749)

In this way, we consecrate our five senses to God as we return to the labor of the coming week.

THE PRAYER FOR THE COMING WEEK

The head of the household usually says a prayer for the coming week at this time. A suggested prayer might be as follows:

Blessed art Thou, our Father, our King who has given us this holy day, a holy calling and your Holy Spirit within us. We thank you, Lord, for calling us out of darkness into your marvelous light. We give you praise for separating us from our sin through the atoning sacrifice of our Messiah Yeshua. Help us, O God, to follow him in this new week, to walk in the light, to walk in love, and to glorify you in our lives. In Yeshua's name we pray. Amen.

One traditional Jewish prayer after the conclusion of havdalah is:

"How beautiful on the mountains are the feet of him who brings good news, proclaiming shalom, bringing good news of good things, announcing salvation and saying to Tziyon, 'Your God is King!'" (Isa. 52:7).

At this point in the ceremony, people can pray spontaneously about the coming week, asking for specific guidance, wisdom, blessings, etc. We serve a God who is concerned about every detail of our lives. He hears and answers our prayers and this is a particularly good time to pray together.

SINGING

Eliyahu Ha-navi is traditionally sung after the prayer for the new week. Eliyahu Ha-navi (Elijah the Prophet) is the one whom the Jewish people expect to announce the coming of the Messiah (based on Malachi 4:5–6). It is long-held belief in Judaism (*Mashiach, Who? What? Why? How? Where? And When?* by Chaim Kramer, pg. 319) that the Messiah will not come on Shabbat but rather immediately following it. That is why there are strong Messianic overtones in the scripture verses selected for havdalah. Those of us who know Messiah and are familiar with the Word of God also know that Elijah did indeed come before the Messiah in the person of *Yochanan the Immerser,* John the Baptizer (Matt. 17:12).

The same spirit of Elijah that cried out, "Prepare ye the way of the Lord," before the first coming of Messiah, should be upon each one of us as we await his Second Coming. Like Elijah, ours must be a message of repentance and redemption, and the repentance must begin with us.

Instead of (or in addition to) singing, "May the prophet Elijah come soon, in our time, with the Messiah, son of David," we can sing any number of messianic songs about the return of Yeshua.

Havdalah ends with a wish for *Shavua Tov* (Good Week). Psalm 91 can be read at this time as we thank God for his protection during the coming week.

DESSERT

A light dessert is usually served following the havdalah ceremony. This is a great time to connect with family, friends, and guests.

CHAPTER 3

HAVDALAH AND ITS MEANING FOR FOLLOWERS OF YESHUA

Havdalah brings great joy to God's followers and is a cause for celebration. It emphasizes the journey of separation that we have taken, withdrawing from the routine activities of the workweek and entering into that island of time called Shabbat.

The New Covenant scriptures continue this theme of separation. Yeshua is described as "set apart" (Heb. 7:26). Believers in Messiah are called to be separate:

> Therefore ADONAI says, "Go out from their midst; separate yourselves; don't even touch what is unclean. Then I myself will receive you." (2 Cor. 6:17)

Believers have a holy calling:

> But you are a chosen people, the King's *cohanim* [priests], a holy nation, a people for God to possess! Why? In order for you to declare the praises of the One who called you out of darkness into his wonderful light. (1 Pet. 2:9)

In his High Priestly prayer of John 17, Yeshua gave a profound teaching on separation:

> I have given them your word, and the world hated them, because they do not belong to the world—just as I myself do not belong to the world. I don't ask you to take them out of the world, but to protect them from the Evil One. They do not belong to the world, just as I do not belong to the world. Set them apart for holiness by means of the truth–your word is truth. (John 17:14–17)

Within the implements and prayers of havdalah, there is significant symbolism for Messianic Jews. Each element of the ceremony can serve not only as a reminder of our call to holiness as Jews, but also as a marker of our new identity in Messiah.

THE CANDLE – LIGHT AND REDEEMER

The two separate candles lit on Shabbat, symbolizing creation and redemption, become one in havdalah. Think of the significance of this type of candle for believers in Yeshua. In him, creation and redemption become one, as the One who was in the beginning became the eternal sacrifice for sin. We, who have accepted this sacrifice, are new creations, redeemed by the blood of the sacrificial lamb. All those who believe join their candles together to become one in him. This was the greatest desire of Yeshua's heart as expressed in his final prayer, "...that they may all be one. Just as you, Father, are united with me and I with you, I pray that they may be united with us..." (John 17:21). Could it be possible that we, like the havdalah candle, need heat applied to us, as well as the pressure of twisting, so that we too can at last become one with Yeshua and our Father?

The light itself also has important meaning. In traditional rabbinic thought, the candle's light is a symbol of the divine presence in man, as it is written: The human spirit is a lamp of ADONAI; it searches one's inmost being (Prov. 20:27). Our creation in God's image is the spark within us that attracts us to God. This is even truer for those of us who know the Messiah in a personal way. We have a fiery treasure—the *Ruach HaKodesh* (Holy Spirit)—that is a beacon for us so that we can know holiness in our lives and be set apart as believers. It is the seal of his new covenant with us—an assurance of a home in heaven and an eternity in the presence of the Holy One of Israel. The light reminds us of this glorious reality!

Another aspect goes beyond the personal realm and extends to Yeshua's call to see him as Messiah, the source of salvation. Yeshua said, "I am the light of the world; whoever follows me will never walk in darkness but will have the light which gives life" (John 8:12). He went on to command his followers to be lights in a world of darkness:

You are light for the world... let your light shine before people, so that they may see the good things you do and praise your Father in heaven. (Matt. 5:14, 16)

16

The light of the special havdalah candle is a wonderful reminder of Messiah, his light, and our commission to be like him. It is a reminder for us to shout from the rooftops, "Yeshua is the *name* of the Lord. He is our salvation. He is the *light* of the world!" Havdalah is a time when we can rededicate ourselves to this high calling of being a light in a dark world at the start of each new week.

THE CUP – JOY OVERFLOWING

A cup of wine is a traditional symbol of joy in Judaism. During the havdalah ceremony, a Kiddush cup overflows into the saucer beneath, reminding us of what David the psalmist said:

You prepare a table for me, even as my enemies watch;
you anoint my head with oil from an overflowing cup. (Ps. 23:5)

God is the source of overflowing joy in the lives of those who follow him. Not just a little joy, but "joy unspeakable and full of glory"! (1 Peter 1:8) The overflowing cup is also a symbol of the abounding divine blessing that we hope for in the new week to come. It is the "fullness of joy" experience by the Messiah and promised to us in John 15:11, "I have said this to you so that my joy may be in you, and your joy be complete."

The visual image of an overflowing cup of wine lingers with those who have experienced havdalah, long after Shabbat is over. So does the image of the multi-wicked candle being extinguished in the overflow from the cup of wine. For Messianic believers, the havdalah ceremony becomes a reenactment of the atoning death of our Messiah. Yeshua, the Light of the World, was "extinguished" (albeit temporarily) and his blood spilled to pay the price for us. When we celebrate the Lord's Seder or Supper, we remember his death as we partake of the cup of wine, a symbol of both blood and joy. At the same time, we look forward to a future Passover (Matt. 26:29) in Messiah's Kingdom, when our joy will be forever overflowing.

THE SPICE OF TRUE LIFE

The spice box also points to a greater image for Messianic believers. We, as believers in Yeshua, are to be an "aroma of the Messiah" (2 Cor. 2:15) to those who are being saved. Our lives are to testify of the peace, rest, joy, and love of the Lord of the Sabbath. We are to be like a refreshing spice box as we leave the Sabbath and enter into the workweek.

THE TABLE

As we sit at our Sabbath table during havdalah, we are reminded of the king's table mentioned in Song of Solomon 1:12. This is Yeshua's table. It is laden with every good and perfect gift for the children of God. It is also the Shabbat table, the place of rest and peace, where, in the presence of the King, we receive his love and give back to him our devotion. The spikenard at the king's table was a precious aromatic herb used in antiquity to welcome love. Havdalah is a great time to receive and welcome the love of God because his love will be with us through the coming week!

FAITH LIKE A CHILD

Children are central to havdalah. A child holds the lit candle and the spice box. This small detail also holds significance. As messianic believers, we can look at a young child holding the light or the spice box and remember a very important truth of the Kingdom of God:

> Yes! I tell you, whoever does not receive the Kingdom of God like a child will not enter it! (Mark 10:15)

May the Lord give us the grace to have the faith and trust of a child! The involvement of children in the Messianic celebration of Shabbat is also connected with the exhortation found in Deuteronomy 6:6 concerning love for God and his commandments, "...you shall teach them diligently to your children..." Since children learn best when all the senses are involved, havdalah is an excellent teaching tool which leaves a lasting impression on the heart of a child.

Havdalah is a tradition rooted in Messianic faith. The traditional symbols have meaning for those who have adopted the new covenant and celebrate Yeshua as Messiah. These symbols focus our eyes on our relationship with the Lord and provide us with a weekly discipline to examine where our heart resides—in the world or in God.

CHAPTER 4

STORIES FROM THE HAVDALAH EXPERIENCE: THEN AND NOW

Picture the early followers of Yeshua celebrating the end of the Shabbat and the beginning of the new week, as described in Acts 20:7-12. Maybe it happened something like this: Paul gives a word from the Scriptures, starting shortly after sundown on Shabbat as part of what is still called in Israel, *motzei Shabbat*. He speaks until midnight. A young man who is sitting in a window falls asleep. He falls three stories and after everyone rushes to his broken body, they realize he is dead. Paul prays for him and he is restored to life. They are stunned.

The Lord used Paul to work a miracle at that meeting, perhaps a havdalah service. May he do the same for us as we gather around the King's table at the close of the Sabbath. May each of us yield to the Lord as he draws us more fully into his Shabbat, havdalah, and ever-increasing consecration and separation unto him.

HAVDALAH: ALIVE AND WELL TODAY

In our home congregation in Ft. Lauderdale, Florida, we began a congregational havdalah experience where approximately ten adults and five children gathered in the home of one of the members on Saturday night for a potluck dinner followed by havdalah. After the ceremony, the children went off to a separate room to play, while the adults lingered around the table to share about themselves: a brief summary of their childhood, how they came to Messiah and/or Messianic Judaism, their favorite scripture, the greatest spiritual challenge in their lives at the moment, and also what matters they felt needed prayer during the upcoming week. This was a beautiful way to get to know one another on a deeper level, working toward that unity that is so dear to the heart of God.

One young couple in our congregation decided to incorporate the dedication of their first child in their havdalah ceremony. Since the theme of the holy dedication was Leviticus 11:44, "...you shall be holy; for I am holy," the consecration of the baby dovetailed perfectly with the consecration of time emphasized in havdalah. Family and friends, Messianic and traditional Jews and gentiles, were invited to light a candle and read a verse from the Tanakh concerning "light." Other elements were added as well, resulting in a very touching ceremony.

CONCLUSION

Havdalah is like a lovely bow tied on the gift that God gives each week to the people he loves. Although not commanded in the Holy Scriptures, it can be a wonderful *mo'ed,* or "appointed time" with the Messiah. It is also an effective and delightful way to pass on our spiritual heritage to our children, and to share that heritage within our Messianic *mishpochah* (family).

Short, but very sweet! We think you'll really enjoy making havdalah a part of your Shabbat experience.

SONGS FOR HAVDALAH

Behold God Is My Salvation *(Isaiah 12:2)*

By Stuart Dauermann
Used by permission
Integrated Copyright Group

Eliyahu Ha-navi

Translation:
May the prophet Elijah come soon, in our time, with the Messiah, son of David.

21

FOR THE CANDLE AND THE SPICES

A Yemenite (16ᵗʰ-cent.) poem by Sa'adiah

My soul longs for the candle and the spices.
If only you would pour me a cup of wine for Havdalah.

O angels on high, pave a way for me,
clear the path for the bewildered [daughter of Zion]
and open the gates that I may enter.

My heart yearning, I shall lift up my eyes to the Lord,
who provides for my needs day and night.

From the treasures of your goodness,
give me the minimum I need,
For your goodness has no end nor limit.
Rejuvenate my joy, my bread and my blessing,
remove all sorrow, pain and darkness.

Now the days of activity begin once again.
May they be renewed in peace and in goodness. Amen.

THE HAVDALAH

The beauty of the Havdalah, a torch, a lamp of light.
An overflowing cup of joy, perfumed in spice delight.
For like the wicks of Havdalah, we are braided into one.
One together in Messiah, Yeshua David's Son.

Individual spices different yet the same
As we come together in His Holy Name.
What a perfect ending filled up with love and joy
The torch of Havdalah is shining that nothing can destroy.

What a perfect ending as we stand here in His sight
no longer separate, but perfected in Messiah's light.

BIBLIOGRAPHY

Ausubel, Nathan. *The Book of Jewish Knowledge*. New York: Crown Publishers, 1964.

Kasdan, Barney. *God's Appointed Times: A Practical Guide For Understanding and Celebrating the Biblical Holidays*. Clarksville: Messianic Jewish Publishers, 1993.

Donin, Rabbi Hayim Halevy. *To Be a Jew*. New York: Basic Books, Inc., 1972.

Fischer, John. "The Meaning of Havdalah: Anticipating Eternal Shabbat." *The Messianic Times*. Fall, 1992: 6.

Greenberg, Rabbi Sidney. *Likrat Shabbat*. Bridgeport: The Prayer Book Press of Media Judaica, Inc., 1978.

Hertz, Joseph H. *The Authorized Daily Prayer Book*. New York: Block Publishing Company, 1979.

Kolatch, Alfred J. *The Jewish Book of Why*. Middle Village: Jonathan David Publishers, Inc., 1981.

Kramer, Chaim. *Mashiach, Who? What? Why? How? Where? And When?* Monsey: Breslov Research Institute, 1994.

Olitzky, Kerry M. *An Encyclopedia of American Synagogue Ritual*. Westport: Greenwood Press, Inc., 2000.

Roth, Cecil. "Havdalah." *Encyclopaedia Judaica*. Jerusalem Volume 7 (FR-HA). Jerusalem: Keter Publishing House, 1972.

Rubin, Barry and Steffi. *The Sabbath: Entering God's Rest*. Clarksville: Messianic Jewish Publishers, 1998.

Siegel, Richard and Michael Strassfeld. *The First Jewish Catalog*. Philadelphia: Jewish Publication Society of America, 1973.

Strassfeld, Sharon. *The First Jewish Catalog*. Philadelphia: Jewish Publication Society of America, 1973, 1-15.

Zimmerman, Martha. *Celebrate the Feasts*. Minneapolis: Bethany Fellowship, Inc., 1981.

Complete Jewish Bible

Presenting the Word of God as a unified Jewish book, here is an English translation for Jews and non-Jews alike. Names and key terms are presented in easy-to-understand transliterated Hebrew, enabling the reader to pronounce them the way Yeshua (Jesus) did!

Available in Hardback, Paperback, blue Bonded Leather and Large Print (hardback).

God's Appointed Times

A Practical Guide for Understanding and Celebrating the Biblical Holidays

How can the biblical holy days such as Passover/Unleavened Bread and Tabernacles be observed? What do they mean for Christians today? This book provides an easily understandable and hands-on approach. Discusses historical background, traditional Jewish observance, New Testament relevance, and prophetic significance.

God's Appointed Customs

A Messianic Jewish Guide to the Biblical Lifecycle and Lifestyle

Are the biblical/Jewish customs just for Jews? Or can Christians also receive blessings by observing them? This explains how God's appointed customs can be part of anyone's lifestyle, Jew or Gentile. This is especially relevant to believers in the Messiah, since Yeshua (Jesus) himself observed them.

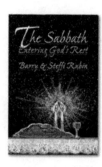

The Sabbath
Entering God's Rest
What is the Sabbath? When is the Sabbath? Should the Sabbath be kept? Whom is the Sabbath for? This book addresses these questions and other controversial aspects surrounding *Shabbat*, the Sabbath. It is a helpful guide for observing the Sabbath, including suggested recipes, blessings and songs. This book will challenge you to have a Sabbath of peace...even into eternity.

Celebrations of the Bible
A Messianic Children's Curriculum
Used by congregations, Sunday schools, homeschoolers and individuals to teach children about the biblical festivals. Each of these holidays are presented for Preschool (2-K), Primary (Grades 1-2), Junior (Grades 4-6), and Children's Worship/Special Services. Our popular curriculum for children is in a brand new user-friendly format. The lay-flat binding allows you to easily reproduce handouts and worksheets.

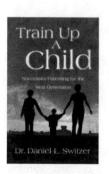

Train Up a Child
Successful Parenting for the Next Generation
The author, former principal of Ets Chaiyim Messianic Jewish Day School, and father of four, combines solid biblical teaching with Jewish sources on child raising giving fresh insight into how parents can disciple their children in the ways of the Lord.

Shabbat & Havdalah Resources

*Available from Messianic Jewish Resources at www.messianicjewish.net
or call 1-800-410-7367.*

Challah Tray – 16"x11.5"
A tradtional Jewish meal begins with the breaking of bread. Challah is a special sweet, golden, egg bread used for Shabbat and holidays.

Kiddush (Blessing) Cup & Saucer
Cup (8.6") Saucer (5.5")

3-piece Shabbat Candlesticks Set
Candlsticks (5.8") and tray (11")

Silverplated Havdalah Set
4-piece set includes tray, kiddush cup, candle holder, and b'samim container.

Havdalah Candles
Set of two candles